51 Bodybuilder Dinner Meals High In Protein:

Increase Muscle Fast Without Pills or Protein Supplements

By

Joseph Correa

Certified Sports Nutritionist

COPYRIGHT

© 2015 Correa Media Group

All rights reserved

Reproduction or translation of any part of this work beyond that permitted by section 107 or 108 of the 1976 United States Copyright Act without the permission of the copyright owner is unlawful.

This publication is designed to provide accurate and authoritative information in regard to

The subject matter covered. It is sold with the understanding that neither the author nor the publisher is engaged in rendering medical advice. If medical advice or assistance is needed, consult with a doctor. This book is considered a guide and should not be used in any way detrimental to your health. Consult with a physician before starting this nutritional plan to make sure it's right for you.

ACKNOWLEDGEMENTS

The realization and success of this book could not have been possible without my family.

51 Bodybuilder Dinner Meals High In Protein:

Increase Muscle Fast Without Pills or Protein Supplements

By

Joseph Correa

Certified Sports Nutritionist

CONTENTS

Copyright

Acknowledgements

About The Author

Introduction

51 Bodybuilder Dinner Meals High In Protein: Increase Muscle Fast Without Pills or Protein Supplements

Other Great Titles by This Author

ABOUT THE AUTHOR

As a certified sports nutritionist and professional athlete, I firmly believe that proper nutrition will help you reach your goals faster and effectively. My knowledge and experience has helped me live healthier throughout the years and which I have shared with family and friends. The more you know about eating and drinking healthier, the sooner you will want to change your life and eating habits.

Being successful in controlling your weight is important as it will improve all aspects of your life.

Nutrition is a key part in the process of getting in better shape and that's what this book is all about.

INTRODUCTION

51 Bodybuilder Dinner Meals High In Protein will help you develop the body you have always wanted by adding more muscle and reducing fat intake. Increasing protein in your diet has been scientifically proven to improve muscle growth and overall performance.

There are many benefits to adding muscle to your body including:

- Increased strength and stamina.
- Improved resistance and training times.
- Quicker recovery after training or competing.
- Look fitter and stronger.
- Develop a more ripped look by increasing muscle size.
- Train longer and harder without getting tired.
- Reduce injuries and muscle cramps.

This book will help you to:

- Prepare better to reach your nutritional goals.

- Have a solid guideline as to how to prepare great meals high in protein.
- Easily choose the recipe that fits your needs for that particular day.
- Create a new habit of eating what your body needs and not what you're forced to eat.

Changing your nutritional habits will change how you look and feel which will give you long lasting results with increased benefits as you age.

The get the most out of your body you need to provide it with the right nutrition and increasing protein in your diet will increase your potential for improvement.

51 BODYBUILDER DINNER MEALS HIGH IN PROTEIN

1. Orange grilled chicken

Ingredients:

3 large chicken breast, boneless and skinless

½ cup of fresh orange juice

1/3 cup of olive oil

2 tsp of lemon juice

3 cloves of garlic, ground

½ tsp of dried thyme

1 tsp of dried oregano

½ tsp of minced cumin

½ tsp of sea salt

Preparation:

First you want to make a marinade. Combine the ingredients in a large plastic bowl, mix well and add chicken. Seal thightly and leave in the refrigerator for about an hour.

Heat up the grill pan over a medium temperature, add chicken and fry for about 15 minutes on each side.

Nutritional values per 100g:

Carbohydrates 17.1g

Sugar 9.5g

Protein 19.3 g

Total fat 6g

Sodium 265.2 mg

Potassium 125.1mg

Calcium 19mg

Iron 8.7mg

Vitamins (vitamin A; B-6; B-12; C; D; D2; D3; K; Riboflavin; Niacin; Thiamin; K)

Calories 154

2. Bacon and beans

Ingredients:

10 slices of bacon

1 cup of green beans, cooked

2 tbsp of dried parsley

1 tsp of mustard

1 tsp of apple vinegar

3 tbsp of olive oil

½ tsp of salt

Preparation:

Fry the bacon in a large saucepan over a medium temperature, until crisp. Cover and set aside. Combine the green beans with mustard, parsley and olive oil. Add bacon and season with salt and apple vinegar.

Refrigerate for about an hour before serving.

Nutritional values per 100g:

Carbohydrates 12.1g

Sugar 6.3g

Protein 14 g

Total fat 4g

Sodium 116.2 mg

Potassium 71.9mg

Calcium 21mg

Iron 7mg

Vitamins (vitamin A; B-6; B-12; C; D; D2; D3; K; Riboflavin; Niacin; Thiamin; K)

Calories 132

3. Lamb cutlets

Ingredients:

4 lamb cutlets, 1/4 inch thick

1 cup of chili beans

3 large red peppers, sliced

1 tbsp of olive oil

½ tsp of sea salt

1tsp of red wine vinegar

Preparation:

Heat up 1 tbsp of olive oil in a large saucepan, over a high temperature. Season the cutlets with sea salt and red wine vinegar. Move to a plate and set aside.

Meanwhile, add the chili beans and red peppers in a saucepan. Fry, stirring occasionally until softened. It should take 5-7 minutes.

Add the cutlets and continue frying for another 15 minutes. Serve the cutlets topped with the bean mixture.

Nutritional values per 100g:

Carbohydrates 14.1g

Sugar 4.5g

Protein 18.9g

Total fat 6g

Sodium 217.1 mg

Potassium 89.1mg

Calcium 29mg

Iron 4mg

Vitamins (vitamin A; B-6; B-12; C; D; D2; D3; K; Riboflavin; Niacin; Thiamin; K)

Calories 143

4. Steak tacos

Ingredients:

1 pound of veal steak

½ cup of fresh lime juice

1 tsp of sea salt

3 cloves of garlic, minced

½ tsp of chili powder

4 tbsp of olive oil

1 small red onion, chopped

3 yellow bell peppers

½ cup of sweet corn

7 small corn tortillas

½ avocado, sliced

¼ cup of soy sauce

2 tbsp of chopped cliantro

Preparation:

First you want to marinate the steak. Combine the lime juice, salt, garlic and chili powder in a large bowl. Add the steak and allow it to stand for about 30 minutes.

Heat up the olive oil in a large skillet over a medium temperature for about 5 minutes. Add the chopped onion and peppers. Cook for about 5-6 minutes. Transfer the vegetables to a plate and set aside.

Now add the steak to a skillet. Reduce heat to medium-low temperature and cook for about 10-15 minutes. Add peppers and mix well. Make tacos with warm tortillas and avocado. Add soy sauce, chopped cliantro and corn. Serve warm.

Nutritional values per 100g:

Carbohydrates 16g

Sugar 11g

Protein 13.5 g

Total fat 5g

Sodium 126mg

Potassium 78.2mg

Calcium 11mg

Iron 4mg

Vitamins (vitamin A; B-6; B-12; C; D; D2; D3; K; Riboflavin; Niacin; Thiamin; K)

Calories 87

5. Avocado rice

Ingredients

3 cups of shrimps, cleaned and frozen

1 medium avocado, ripe

1 ½ cup of cooked brown rice

2 eggs

1 tbsp of honey

2 tsp of olive oil

¼ tsp of red pepper

1 tbsp of red wine vinegar

2 tbsp of sesame seeds

1 cup of red beans

Preparation:

Heat up the olive oil in a large saucepan over a medium temperature. Add honey and stir well until it melts. Now add the shrimps and fry well for few minutes on each side. Season with pepper and remove from the saucepan. Use the same saucepan to fry eggs for about 2 minutes. Transfer to a plate and cut into strips.

In a small bowl, combine the rice with red wine vinegar and red beans. Top with egg strips, shrimps and avocado slices.

Nutritional values per 100g:

Carbohydrates 28.2g

Sugar 13.1g

Protein 32.1 g

Total fat 11g

Sodium 621.4 mg

Potassium 119mg

Calcium 31mg

Iron 7mg

Vitamins (vitamin A; B-6; B-12; C; D; D2; D3; K; Riboflavin; Niacin; Thiamin; K)

Calories 181

6. Lemon chicken

Ingredients:

4 chicken breast halves, skinless and boneless

½ cup of chicken broth

2 tbsp of dry parsley, chopped

2 tbsp of walnuts, minced

1 tbsp of fresh lemon juice

¼ tsp of lemon zest

2 tsp of rice flour

½ tsp of sea salt

¼ tsp of black pepper

2 tbsp of olive oil

1 medium onion, chopped

1 cup of brown rice, cooked

Preparation:

Combine parsley, walnuts and lemon zest in a bowl. Wash and pat dry the chicken. Dust with the flour, salt and pepper.

Use a large saucepan to heat up the olive oil over a medium temperature. Add the chopped onion and fry for about 3-4 minutes. Stir well and add the chicken breast. Fry until golden color.

Now pour the chicken broth and lemon juice over the chicken. Cover and let it cook for about 20 minutes on a very low temperature. Stir in the parsley mixture and remove from the heat. Serve warm.

Nutritional values per 100g:

Carbohydrates 28g

Sugar 10.5g

Protein 30.1 g

Total fat 9.9g

Sodium 611.3 mg

Potassium 103 mg

Calcium 19mg

Iron 7.6mg

Vitamins (vitamin A; B-6; B-12; C; D; D2; D3; K; Riboflavin; Niacin; Thiamin; K)

Calories 177

7. Spinach pizza

Ingredients:

1 medium whole wheat pizza crust

¼ cup of sugar free pizza sauce

½ cup of chopped spinach

½ small onion, chopped

1 cup of cottage cheese

½ cup of button mushrooms, sliced

¼ cup of ricotta, skim

2 tbsp of grated parmesan cheese

1 tbsp of olive oil

Preparation:

Preheat the oven to 350 degrees. Lay the pizza crust on a baking sheet. Spread the sauce over the pizza crust. Now add the spinach and the onions. Sprinkle with cottage cheese and mushrooms and make a final layer with ricota and parmesan. Drizzle the olive oil.

Bake for about 10 mintes, cut and serve.

Nutritional values per 100g:

Carbohydrates 29.2g

Sugar 16.1g

Protein 32.2 g

Total fat 10g

Sodium 611.4 mg

Potassium 102mg

Calcium 22mg

Iron 5.7mg

Vitamins (vitamin A; B-6; B-12; C; D; D2; D3; K; Riboflavin; Niacin; Thiamin; K)

Calories 171

8. Broccoli and ricotta pasta

Ingredients:

1 cup of whole wheat pasta

1 cup of cooked broccoli

¼ cup of skim ricotta

1 cup of chopped lean sausages

2 tbsp of parmesan cheese, grated

¼ tsp of salt

2 tbsp of olive oil

1 small onion, sliced

1 clove of garlic, ground1/2 medium red onion, thinly sliced

1 garlic clove, sliced

Small pinch crushed red pepper flakes

2 tablespoons tomato paste

Preparation:

Pour 3 cups of water in a large pot. Bring it to boil and add broccoli. Cook for about 10 minutes until soft. Remove from the water and allow it to cool. Chop into bite-size pieces.

Now add the pasta into the same pot and use a package instructions to cook it.

Meanwhile, heat the olive oil in a large saucepan, over a medium temperature. Add the chopped sausages, onion slices, garlic, and red pepper. Cook for about 8 minutes, stiring occasionally. Add cooked broccoli and mix well until tender. Pour in the tomato sauce and cook for another minute.

Reduce heat to minimum and add pasta. Add some water if the mixture seems dry. Stir in skim ricotta and parmesan cheese. Serve warm.

Nutritional values per 100g:

Carbohydrates 26g

Sugar 11g

Protein 28.3 g

Total fat 9g

Sodium 421.1 mg

Potassium 128.1mg

Calcium 19mg

Iron 8.7mg

Vitamins (vitamin A; B-6; B-12; C; D; D2; D3; K; Riboflavin; Niacin; Thiamin; K)

Calories 186

9. Roast veggies with goat's cheese

Ingredients:

½ cup of beetroot, peeled and diced

½ cup of green beans, cooked and drained

½ cup of brussel sprouts, chopped

½ cup of pumpkin, peeled and chopped

½ cup of carrot, chopped

1 cup of fresh tomatoes, roughly chopped

½ cup of roasted tomatoes

1 small onion, sliced

½ cup of cooked lentils

2 garlic cloves, minced

1 cup of finely chopped silverbeet

salt and pepper to taste

3 tbsp of olive oil

1 cup of crumbled goat's cheese

Preparation:

Preheat the oven to 350 degrees. In a large bowl, combine beetroot, green beans, brussel sprouts and pumpkin. Add 1 tbsp of olive oil and some salt to taste. Place on an oven tray and bake for about 20 minutes.

Meanwhile, heatup the remaining oil in a medium sized saucepan. Add onions and carrot and fry for about 5 minutes, stirring constantly.

Add diced tomatoes and silverbeet. Season with pepper and gently simmer for about 20 minutes. give a stir then add silverbeet, salt and pepper.

Serve the lentils topped with roasted vegetables, roasted tomatoes and goat's cheese.

Nutritional values per 100g:

Carbohydrates 32.7g

Sugar 14g

Protein 34 g

Total fat 12.7g

Sodium 645 mg

Potassium 141.2mg

Calcium 23mg

Iron 7mg

Vitamins (vitamin A; B-6; B-12; C; D; D2; D3; K; Riboflavin; Niacin; Thiamin; K)

Calories 204

10. Thai tofu with ginger

Ingredients:

1 cup of tofu, chopped into cubes

3 tbsp of ginger sauce

1 tbsp of olive oil

2 tbsp of fresh ginger, ground

2 cloves of garlic

2 tbsp of minced fresh chili peppers

½ cup of fresh button mushrooms

1 cup of fresh yellow pepper, chopped

1 cup of green beans, cooked

2 tbsp of teriyaki sauce

¼ cup of water

¼ cup of fresh basil, chopped

1 small onion, peeled and sliced

2 cups of brown rice, boiled

Preparation:

Combine the ingredients in a non-stick frying pan or a wok. Heat up the stove to a medium temperature and fry the ingredients for about 20 minutes, stirring constantly.

Serve with brown rice.

Nutritional values per 100g:

Carbohydrates 29g

Sugar 12.1g

Protein 30.1 g

Total fat 11.9g

Sodium 522.1 mg

Potassium 104.9mg

Calcium 32mg

Iron 8.6mg

Vitamins (vitamin A; B-6; B-12; C; D; D2; D3; K; Riboflavin; Niacin; Thiamin; K)

Calories 157

11. White bean peperonata

Ingredients:

2 tbsp of olive oil

1 small onion, sliced

2 cloves of garlic, chopped

1 red capsicum, chopped

2 small tomatoes, sliced

1 cup of green beans

1 tbsp of apple vinegar

2 tbsp of olive oil

few basil leaves for decoration

salt and pepper to taste

Preparation:

Heat up the olive oil in a large saucepan over medium heat. Add sliced onion and fry for few minutes, until golden color. Add garlic and capsicum, season with salt and pepper. Fry for 15 minutes, stirring constantly.

Reduce the heat to low and add tomatoes and green beans. Cover and cook for few minutes. Remove from the heat and serve.

Nutritional values per 100g:

Carbohydrates 28.2g

Sugar 14.5g

Protein 33.5 g

Total fat 12g

Sodium 626.5 mg

Potassium 121.2mg

Calcium 34mg

Iron 10mg

Vitamins (vitamin A; B-6; B-12; C; D; D2; D3; K; Riboflavin; Niacin; Thiamin; K)

Calories 197

12. Pumpkin and chickpea salad

Ingredients:

2 cups of chopped pumpkin

2 tsp of fresh cumin

2 tsp of ground coriander

4 tbsp of vegetable oil

1 cup of chickpeas, drained

8 dried figs, sliced

1 red onion, sliced

¼ cup of fresh coriander, chopped

4 tbsp of fresh lemon juice

¼ cup of olive oil

Preparation:

Preheat the oven to 300 degrees.

In a large bowl, combine the pumpkin with cumin, coriander and vegetable. Mix well. Sperad this pumpkin mixture on a baking sheet and bake for about 20 minutes. Remove from the oven and allow it to cool.

Place pumpkin, chickpeas, figs, onion, coriander leaves, lemon rind, lemon juice and olive oil into a bowl and toss gently to coat. Serve.

Nutritional values per 100g:

Carbohydrates 26g

Sugar 12.5g

Protein 32.5 g

Total fat 7g

Sodium 612 mg

Potassium 84.1mg

Calcium 31mg

Iron 9mg

Vitamins (vitamin A; B-6; B-12; C; D; D2; D3; K; Riboflavin; Niacin; Thiamin; K)

Calories 179

13. Feta frittata

Ingredients:

2 cups of chopped kale

3 tbsp of olive oil

1 medium Italian sausage, sliced

1 small onion, peeled and sliced

6 eggs, lightly beaten

½ cup of feta cheese

¼ tsp of salt

Preparation:

Boil kale for about 5 minutes. Drain and squeeze out as much liquid as possible. Slice roughly.

Heat up the olive oil in a large saucepan. Fry sausage slices for about 3 minutes, turning often. Add onions and fry for another 2-3 minutes. Add kale and stir well. Season with salt. Pour over the beaten eggs, mix with a fork and remove from heat after about a minute.

Crumble feta cheese on top and serve warm.

Nutritional values per 100g:

Carbohydrates 16g

Sugar 3.5g

Protein 20.5 g

Total fat 5.7g

Sodium 518.1 mg

Potassium 83.1mg

Calcium 31.4mg

Iron 7mg

Vitamins (vitamin A; B-6; B-12; C; D; D2; D3; K; Riboflavin; Niacin; Thiamin; K)

Calories 160

14. Crustless quiche

Ingredients:

1 small onion, chopped

4 large slices of bacon

4 eggs

1 tbsp of dry parsley, chopped

¼ cup of rice flour

1 tbsp of almond butter

2 cups of skim milk

½ tsp of salt

¼ tsp of pepper

Preparation:

In a large bowl, whisk together eggs and milk. Add rice flour and butter. Mix well with an electric mixer. Add other ingredients and pour this mixture into a baking dish.

Preheat oven to 300 degrees and bake for about 30 minutes.

Nutritional values per 100g:

Carbohydrates 19.2g

Sugar 7.5g

Protein 29.5 g

Total fat 11g

Sodium 531 mg

Potassium 63mg

Calcium 31.2mg

Iron 9.1mg

Vitamins (vitamin A; B-6; B-12; C; D; D2; D3; K; Riboflavin; Niacin; Thiamin; K)

Calories 177

15. Grilled lamb and vegetables

Ingredients:

3 medium lamb fillets

2 tbsp of olive oil

½ tsp of ground cumin

1 clove of garlic, ground

½ tsp of sea salt

¼ tsp of black pepper

1 medium yellow pepper, chopped

1 medium eggplant, peeled and sliced

1 cucumber, peeled and sliced

2 tbsp of fresh parsley, chopped

Preparation:

Heat up the olive oil in a large saucepan over a high temperature. Slice eggplant lengthwise and fry for few minutes. Reduce the heat and add other vegetables. Season with salt, pepper and cumin. Cover the saucepan and cook for about 15 minutes, stirring occasionally.

Preheat the oven to 350 degrees. In a medium sized baking pan, spread the vegetables to make an even layer. Put the lamb fillets on top and bake for 30 minutes.

Nutritional values per 100g:

Carbohydrates 16g

Sugar 7.5g

Protein 26.5 g

Total fat 10g

Sodium 531.2 mg

Potassium 63.1mg

Calcium 31mg

Iron 6mg

Vitamins (vitamin A; B-6; B-12; C; D; D2; D3; K; Riboflavin; Niacin; Thiamin; K)

Calories 201

16. BBQ pork ribs

Ingredients:

1 pound of pork ribs

3 tbsp of olive oil

½ cup of fresh tomato sauce

¼ cup of sugar free barbecue sauce

2 cloves of garlic, ground

¼ cup of brown sugar

1 tsp of Tabasco sauce

Preparation:

First you want to prepare the marinade. In a large bowl, combine fresh tomato sauce, barbecue sauce, Tabasco sauce, brown sugar and garlic. Place pork ribs into the marinade, coat well and leave in the refrigerator for about an hour.

Spread the olive oil over the grill pan. Fry the ribs for about 10 minutes on each side.

Nutritional values per 100g:

Carbohydrates 22 g

Sugar 6.5g

Protein 26.5 g

Total fat 11g

Sodium 468 mg

Potassium 82.1mg

Calcium 20mg

Iron 6.5mg

Vitamins (vitamin A; B-6; B-12; C; D; D2; D3; K; Riboflavin; Niacin; Thiamin; K)

Calories 181

17. Sausage salad

Ingredients:

8 thick beef sausages (gluten-free)

1 medium potato, boiled

1 red onion, peeled and sliced

3 tbsp of extra virgin olive oil

salt and pepper to taste

1 tsp of vinegar

Preparation:

Heat up the olive oil in a large frypan over a high temperature. Fry sausages for about 4 minutes. Remove from the pan and allow it to cool for about 30 minutes. Cut into slices and combine with potato and red onion. Season with salt, pepper and vinegar. Let it stand in the refrigerator for about 30 minutes before serving.

Nutritional values per 100g:

Carbohydrates 15 g

Sugar 2.5g

Protein 27.5 g

Total fat 11g

Sodium 531.1 mg

Potassium 82.1mg

Calcium 11mg

Iron 5mg

Vitamins (vitamin A; B-6; B-12; C; D; D2; D3; K; Riboflavin; Niacin; Thiamin; K)

Calories 136

18. Barbecued salmon with asparagus

Ingredients:

4 thick salmon fillets

¼ cup of non fat mayonnaise

1 cup of asparagus, chopped

1 tbsp of basil, chopped

1 tbsp coriander, chopped

2 tbsp olive oil

Preparation:

Combine the mayonnaise with basil and coriander. Mix well and set aside.

Heat up the olive oil in a medium saucepan over medium-high temperature. Fry salmon fillets for about 3 minutes on each side. Remove from the saucepan. Add chopped asparagus to the same saucepan. Reduce the heat to medium and fry for about 5 minutes, stirring occasionally.

Serve asparagus with salmon and mayonnaise.

Nutritional values per 100g:

Carbohydrates 19.1g

Sugar 5.5g

Protein 23.5 g

Total fat 5g

Sodium 538.7 mg

Potassium 85.2mg

Calcium 32mg

Iron 9.9mg

Vitamins (vitamin A; B-6; B-12; C; D; D2; D3; K; Riboflavin; Niacin; Thiamin; K)

Calories 147

19. Chicken with almonds

Ingredients:

5 pieces of chicken thighs, boneless and skinless

3 medium red onions, sliced

3 medium sweet potatoes, cut into thick slices

2 red peppers, sliced

2 cloves of garlic, chopped

3 tbsp of olive oil

2 tbsp of fresh lemon juice

4 tbsp of almonds, chopped

1 cup of Greek yogurt

1 tbsp of fresh parsley, chopped

Preparation:

Preheat the oven to 300 degrees. In a large bowl, combine chicken thighs with onions, potato slices and peppers. Transfer to a baking sheet. In another bowl, mix together garlic, olive oil, fresh lemon juice and almonds. Pour this mixture over the meat and bake for about 40 minutes.

Remove from the oven and allow it to cool well. Serve in small bowls topped with Greek yogurt and parsley.

Nutritional values per 100g:

Carbohydrates 26g

Sugar 9.5g

Protein 31.5 g

Total fat 11g

Sodium 598.1 mg

Potassium 93.2mg

Calcium 21mg

Iron 7.8mg

Vitamins (vitamin A; B-6; B-12; C; D; D2; D3; K; Riboflavin; Niacin; Thiamin; K)

Calories 197

20. Ricotta omelet

Ingredients:

4 eggs

2 tbsp of dried parsley

1 small clove of garlic

2 tbsp of Parmesan cheese

2 tbsp of olive oil

½ cup of ricotta

1 tsp of fresh basil, chopped

Preparation:

Beat the eggs and mix well with parsley, garlic, parmesan, ricotta and basil. Heat up the olive oil over a high temperature. Fry the eggs for about 3-4 minutes, stirring constantly. Serve immediately.

Nutritional values per 100g:

Carbohydrates 21g

Sugar 7.2g

Protein 25.1 g

Total fat 7g

Sodium 668.2 mg

Potassium 73.7mg

Calcium 22mg

Iron 8mg

Vitamins (vitamin A; B-6; B-12; C; D; D2; D3; K; Riboflavin; Niacin; Thiamin; K)

Calories 173

21. Chicken kebap

Ingredients:

2 small potatoes, peeled and cut into thin slices

2 chicken breast, boneless and skinless, cut into cubes

1 medium red onion, sliced

1 red pepper, sliced

3 tbsp each of chopped parsley, mint and chives

2 small tomatoes, sliced

6 tbsp of olive oil

For the marinade:

2 tbsp of lemon juice

2 green chillies, seeded and finely chopped

2 small garlic cloves, finely chopped

4 tbsp of olive oil

2 tbsp white wine vinegar

Preparation:

Boil the potatoes for about 20 minutes, until soften. Drain and allow it to cool. In a large bowl mix the lemon juice, green chillies, chopped garlic cloves, olive oil and vinegar. Soak the meat and the vegetables into this marinade and let it stand in the refrigerator for at least one hour.

Arrange the meat and vegetables on a wooden sticks. Use a kitchen brush to spread the remaining olive oil over the chicken kebaps. Barbecue directly over a medium temperature for about 5-6 minutes on each side.

Nutritional values per 100g:

Carbohydrates 29.1g

Sugar 16.1g

Protein 33 g

Total fat 12g

Sodium 521.4 mg

Potassium 84.1mg

Calcium 21mg

Iron 8mg

Vitamins (vitamin A; B-6; B-12; C; D; D2; D3; K; Riboflavin; Niacin; Thiamin; K)

Calories 243

22. Spiced eggs

Ingredients:

4 eggs, beaten

1 small onion, chopped

1 small chilli pepper, chopped

1 tbsp of butter

¼ cup of skim milk

1 small tomato, chopped

1 tsp of dry coriander leaves

Preparation:

Melt the butter over a medium heat. Add onion and chili and fry for about 5 minutes, until soften. Now add tomato, stir well and fry until the water evaporates. Meanwhile, combine the eggs with milk and dry coriander leaves. Pour this mixture into the frying pan and fry for another 2-3 minutes.

Nutritional values per 100g:

Carbohydrates 18g

Sugar 7.5g

Protein 20 g

Total fat 6g

Sodium 462.1 mg

Potassium 53.2mg

Calcium 30mg

Iron 9.6mg

Vitamins (vitamin A; B-6; B-12; C; D; D2; D3; K; Riboflavin; Niacin; Thiamin; K)

Calories 127

23. Chili salmon

Ingredients:

4 thick slices of salmon fillets, cut into madium cubes

4 tbsp of chilli sauce

2 tbsp of fresh lime juice

3 tbsp of vegetable oil

Preparation:

Combine the sweet chilli sauce and lime juice in a bowl. Soak the salmon fillets into this mixture and allow it to stand for about 30 minutes. Heat up the oil over a high temperature. Fry the fillets for about 8 minutes. Remove from the pan and use a kitchen paper to soak the excess oil. Serve warm.

Nutritional values per 100g:

Carbohydrates 16.1g

Sugar 8.5g

Protein 24.1 g

Total fat 5.3g

Sodium 511.1 mg

Potassium 82.1mg

Calcium 23mg

Iron 4mg

Vitamins (vitamin A; B-6; B-12; C; D; D2; D3; K; Riboflavin; Niacin; Thiamin; K)

Calories 151

24. Bacon with mushrooms

Ingredients:

1 pound of bacon, sliced

1 cup of fresh button mushrooms

4 eggs, beaten

1 cup of cherry tomatoes, halved

½ cup of cottage cheese

1 tbsp of dry parsley

3 tbsp of oil for frying

Preparation:

Fry the bacon over a medium-high temperature for about 5 minutes on each side. Reduce the heat to low and add tomatoes, mushrooms and eggs. Season with parsley and cover. Fry for about 6-7 more minutes. Remove from the heat and serve warm.

Nutritional values per 100g:

Carbohydrates 10.g

Sugar 2.5g

Protein 23.5 g

Total fat 11g

Sodium 534.2 mg

Potassium 81.2mg

Calcium 32mg

Iron 7mg

Vitamins (vitamin A; B-6; B-12; C; D; D2; D3; K; Riboflavin; Niacin; Thiamin; K)

Calories 170

25. Salmon and green beans mix

Preparation:

3 large salmon fillets, skinless

1 cup of green beans

½ cup of lentils

1 egg

1 tbsp of fresh lemon juice

2 tbsp of olive oil

½ cup of green onions, chopped

Preparation:

Boil the egg for 10 minutes. Remove from the pot, allow it to cool and peel. Cut the egg into the small cubes. Set aside.

Wash and drain green beans and lentils. Mix with the egg.

Heat up the olive oil over a medium temperature. Fry the salmon fillets for about 5 minutes on each side. Remove from the pan and use the kitchen paper to soak up the excess oil. Let it stand for a while and cut into small cubes.

In a large bowl, combine the salmon cubes with onions and egg mixture. Allow it to stand in the refrigerator for about 30 minutes before serving.

Nutritional values per 100g:

Carbohydrates 18.3g

Sugar 5.5g

Protein 20.5 g

Total fat 3.4g

Sodium 390.2 mg

Potassium 53mg

Calcium 22mg

Iron 7mg

Vitamins (vitamin A; B-6; B-12; C; D; D2; D3; K; Riboflavin; Niacin; Thiamin; K)

Calories 114

26. Couscous

Ingredients:

1 cup of instant couscous

2 large carrots

½ tsp of dried rosemary

1 cup of green beans, cooked and drained

10 green olives, pitted

1 tbsp of lemon juice

1 tbsp of orange juice

1 tbsp of orange zest

4 tbsp of olive oil

½ tsp of salt

Preparation:

Wash and peel carrots. Cut into thin slices. Heat up 2 tbsp of olive oil in a large pan over medium heat. Add carrots and cook, stirring constantly. It should be tender after about 10-15 minutes. Add rosemary, green beans, olives and orange juice. Mix well. Continue to cook and stir occasionally.

Combine lemon juice with 1 cup of water. Add this mixture to a saucepan and mix with 2 tbsp of olive oil, orange zest and salt. Allow it to boil and add couscous. Remove from heat and allow it to stand for about 15 minutes.

Pour these two mixtures into a large bowl and mix well with a tablespoon.

Nutritional values per 100g:

Carbohydrates 29g

Sugar 14.2g

Protein 31 g

Total fat 13g

Sodium 602 mg

Potassium 97mg

Calcium 33mg

Iron 11mg

Vitamins (vitamin A; B-6; B-12; C; D; D2; D3; K; Riboflavin; Niacin; Thiamin; K)

Calories 202

27. Chicken with avocado

Ingredients:

1 large piece of chicken breast, boneless and skinless, cooked

1 cup of green beans

½ of ripe avocado, peeled and chopped

¼ of cucumber, peeled, deseeded and chopped

1 tsp of Tabasco sauce

2 tbsp of fresh lemon juice

2 tbsp of extra-virgin olive oil

few lettuce leaves

1 tbsp of mixed seeds

Preparation:

Cut the chicken into medium sized cubes. Fry for about 5 minutes in preheated pan, stiring constantly. Remove from the pan and set aside.

Meanwhile, combine the green beans, avocado chops, cucumber, Tabasco sauce, lettuce and lemon juice in a blender. Mix well for about 30-40 seconds. Pour this mixture over chicken cubes and let it stand in the refrigerator for at least 30 minutes before serving.

Nutritional values per 100g:

Carbohydrates 24g

Sugar 11.5g

Protein 29.5 g

Total fat 10g

Sodium 462.1 mg

Potassium 63.1mg

Calcium 11mg

Iron 5.6mg

Vitamins (vitamin A; B-6; B-12; C; D; D2; D3; K; Riboflavin; Niacin; Thiamin; K)

Calories 165

28. Grilled avocado in curry sauce

Ingredients:

1 large avocado, chopped

¼ cup of water

1 tbsp of ground curry

2 tbsp of olive oil

1 tsp of soy sauce

1 tsp of chopped parsley

¼ tsp of red pepper

¼ tsp of sea salt

Preparation:

Heat up olive oil in a large saucepan, over a medium temperature. In a small bowl, combine ground curry, soy sauce, chopped parsley, red pepper and sea salt. Add water and cook for about 5 minutes, over a medium temperature. Add chopped avocado, stir well and cook for another few minutes, until all the liquid evaporates. Turn off the heat and cover. Let it stand for about 15-20 minutes before serving.

Nutritional values per 100g:

Carbohydrates 9.8g

Sugar 2.5g

Protein 24 g

Total fat 3g

Sodium 112 mg

Potassium 24mg

Calcium 12mg

Iron 2.3mg

Vitamins (vitamin A; B-6; B-12; C; D; D2; D3; K; Riboflavin; Niacin; Thiamin; K)

Calories 143

29. Tofu fried vegetables

Ingredients:

½ cup of soft tofu

1 small onion

1 small carrot

1 small tomato

2 medium red peppers

salt to taste

1 tbsp of olive oil

Preparation:

Wash and pat dry the vegetables using a kitchen paper. Cut into thin slices or strips. Heat up the olive oil over a medium temperature and fry the vegetables for about 10 minutes, stirring constantly. Add salt and mix well. You want to wait until the vegetables soften, then add soft tofu. Stir well. Fry for another 2-3 minutes. Remove from the heat and serve.

Nutritional values per 100g:

Carbohydrates 27g

Sugar 6.5g

Protein 29.5 g

Total fat 11g

Sodium 611 mg

Potassium 72mg

Calcium 27mg

Iron 6.7mg

Vitamins (vitamin A; B-6; B-12; C; D; D2; D3; K; Riboflavin; Niacin; Thiamin; K)

Calories 198

30. Leek with seitan cubes

Ingredients:

2 cups of trimmed leeks

1 cup of seitan, cut into cubes

olive oil

thyme leaves for decoration

salt and red pepper to taste

Preparation:

Cut the leeks into small pieces and wash it under cold water, day before serving. Leave it overnight in a plastic bag.

Heat the oil in a large pan, over a medium temperature. Add seitan cubes and fry for about 15 minutes. Add leaks, mix well and fry for another 10 minutes on a low temperature. Remove from the saucepan and allow it to cool. Decorate with thyme leaves. Add salt and pepper to taste.

Nutritional values per 100g:

Carbohydrates 11g

Sugar 6.5g

Protein 17.1 g

Total fat 6g

Sodium 232.1 mg

Potassium 53.1mg

Calcium 32mg

Iron 4mg

Vitamins (vitamin A; B-6; B-12; C; D; D2; D3; K; Riboflavin; Niacin; Thiamin; K)

Calories 124

31. Eggplant casserole

Ingredients:

2 large eggplants

1 cup of tempeh, sliced

1 medium onion

2 tbsp of oil

¼ tsp of pepper

2 small tomatoes

1 tbsp of dried parsley

½ cup of soft tofu, pureed

3 tbsp of bread crumbs

1 cup of non fat milk

½ cup of non fat milk cream

Preparation:

Grease the baking pan with oil. Preheat the oven at 350 degrees. Peel the eggplants and cut them lengthwise into thin slices. Layer eggplant slices in a baking pan. Peel and cut the onion and tomatoes into thin slices. Make another layer in a baking pan. Spread the tempeh slices on top.

Combine bread crumbs with non fat milk, pureed soft tofu, soy cream, parsley and pepper in a large bowl. Whisk well until smooth mixture. Pour this mixture on top of your casserole and bake for about 20 minutes.

Cut into 6 equal pieces and serve.

Nutritional values per 100g:

Carbohydrates 17.1g

Sugar 3.5g

Protein 20.5 g

Total fat 5g

Sodium 568mg

Potassium 81.2mg

Calcium 30mg

Iron 5.1mg

Vitamins (vitamin A; B-6; B-12; C; D; D2; D3; K; Riboflavin; Niacin; Thiamin; K)

Calories 177

32. Salmon with cucumber sauce

Ingredients:

4 salmon fillets, sliced

1 cup of whole wheat orzo, cooked

1 large cucumber, peeled and chopped

2 tsp of olive oil

½ tsp of ground cumin

1 tsp of brown sugar

½ tsp of black pepper

½ tsp of sea salt

1 cup of Greek yogurt

1 scallion, finely chopped

1 tsp of fresh lemon juice

Preparation:

Combine the olive oil, cumin, brown sugar, pepper and salt in a bowl. Put the salmon on a baking sheet and coat with this mixture. Allow it to stand in the refrigerator for about 20 minutes.

Preheat the oven to 350 degrees. In a small bowl, mix the Greek yogurt with cucumber, scallion, parsley and lemon juice. Bake the salmon for about 7-10 minutes and serve over the orzo, topped with the Greek yogurt sauce.

Nutritional values per 100g:

Carbohydrates 27g

Sugar 11g

Protein 26.7 g

Total fat 8g

Sodium 598 mg

Potassium 92.1mg

Calcium 41mg

Iron 11mg

Vitamins (vitamin A; B-6; B-12; C; D; D2; D3; K; Riboflavin; Niacin; Thiamin; K)

Calories 182

33. Seitan burritos

Ingredients:

1 cup of cooked green beans

1 pound of seitan, chopped

1 cup of soft tofu

½ cup of chopped onions

1 tsp of ground red pepper

1 tsp of chili powder

6 whole grain tortillas

Preparation:

Combine seitan with ground red pepper, chili powder and onions in a frying pan. Stir well for 15 minutes on a low temperature. Remove from the heat.

Mix soft tofu with green beans in a blender. Mix well for about 30 seconds. Add the tofu mixture to the seitan. Divide this mixture into 6 equal pieces and spread over tortillas. Wrap and serve.

Nutritional values per 100g:

Carbohydrates 19g

Sugar 7.5g

Protein 17 g

Total fat 4.3g

Sodium 188mg

Potassium 72 mg

Calcium 27mg

Iron 5.9mg

Vitamins (vitamin A; B-6; B-12; C; D; D2; D3; K; Riboflavin; Niacin; Thiamin; K)

Calories 123

34. Chickpea Tagine

Ingredients:

4 small tomatoes, chopped

1 medium onion, sliced

1 medium zuccini, chopped

1 cup of dry apricots

2 tbsp of olive oil

½ tsp of sea salt

2 small carrots, sliced lengthwise

2 cloves of garlic, ground

2 tbsp of ginger, minced

2 tsp of honey

1 tsp of cumin, ground

1 tsp of cinnamon, ground

¼ tsp of turmeric

½ cup of water

2 cups of chickpeas, drained

2 tbsp of fresh lemon juice

1 cup of whole wheat couscous, cooked

3 tbsp of almonds, minced

Preparation:

Warm up the olive oil over a medium temperature in a large saucepan. Add the onions and salt. Fry for about 5 minutes, stirring occasionally. Now add the carrots and fry for another 5 minutes.

Now add the spices and raise the heat. Stir well and add tomatoes, zucchini and apricots. Pour in the water and bring it to boil. Cover and reduce the heat. Simmer gently for about 20 minutes.

Now you have to add chickpeas and lemon juice. Cook uncovered until the chickpeas are done and the water evaporates. Melt in the honey and remove from the heat. Serve with couscous and garnish with almonds.

Nutritional values per 100g:

Carbohydrates 22.7g

Sugar 7.1g

Protein 19g

Total fat 7.4g

Sodium 570 mg

Potassium 71.2mg

Calcium 35.3mg

Iron 8mg

Vitamins (vitamin A; B-6; B-12; C; D; D2; D3; K; Riboflavin; Niacin; Thiamin; K)

Calories 167

35. Chia seeds bread

Ingredients:

3 cups of buckwheat flour

½ cup of pumpkin puree

1 cup of minced chia seeds

warm water

salt

½ pack of dry yeast

Preparation:

Mix flour, pumpkin puree and chia seeds with salt and yeast. Add warm water and stir until smooth dough. Let it stand in a warm place for about 30-40 minutes. Sprinkle with cold water and bake in preheated oven, at 350 degrees for about 40 minutes, until nice gold brown color. Remove from the oven, cover with a kitchen napkin and allow it to cool.

Nutritional values per 100g:

Carbohydrates 17.2g

Sugar 3.5g

Protein 21.5 g

Total fat 5g

Sodium 528.1 mg

Potassium 84.1mg

Calcium 30mg

Iron 9mg

Vitamins (vitamin A; B-6; B-12; C; D; D2; D3; K; Riboflavin; Niacin; Thiamin; K)

Calories 171

36. Grilled green peppers

Ingredients:

2 green peppers

3 tbsp of olive oil

2 cloves of garlic

chopped parsley

1 tbsp of soy sauce

¼ tsp of sea salt

¼ tsp of pepper

Preparation:

First you want to prepare the sauce. In a small bowl, combine 3 tbsp of olive oil with garlic, chopped parsley, soy sauce, salt and pepper. Mix well. Spread the sauce over peppers and fry in a barbecue pan on a medium temperature for about 10-15 minutes. Stir constantly.

Serve warm.

Nutritional values per 100g:

Carbohydrates 22.3g

Sugar 6.2g

Protein 23 g

Total fat 7g

Sodium 382.6 mg

Potassium 52mg

Calcium 21mg

Iron 5mg

Vitamins (vitamin A; B-6; B-12; C; D; D2; D3; K; Riboflavin; Niacin; Thiamin; K)

Calories 175

37. Zucchini slices with garlic

Ingredients:

1 large zucchini

4 cloves of garlic

1 tbsp of olive oil

¼ tsp of salt

Preparation:

Peel and cut zucchini into thick slices. Chop garlic and fry it for few minutes in olive oil, until nice gold color. Add zucchini and fry for another 10 minutes on a medium temperature. Sprinkle with some chopped parsley before serving. Salt to taste.

Nutritional values per 100g:

Carbohydrates 21.7g

Sugar 9.5g

Protein 28 g

Total fat 5g

Sodium 571.3 mg

Potassium 92.3mg

Calcium 40mg

Iron 9.8mg

Vitamins (vitamin A; B-6; B-12; C; D; D2; D3; K; Riboflavin; Niacin; Thiamin; K)

Calories 181

38. Baked mushrooms in tomato sauce

Ingredients:

1 cup of button mushrooms

1 large tomato

3 tbsp of olive oil

2 cloves of garlic

1 tbsp of fresh basil

salt and pepper to taste

Preparation:

Wash and peel tomato. Cut in small pieces. Chop garlic and mix with tomato and fresh basil. Heat up the olive oil in a saucepan and put tomato in it. Add ¼ cup of water, mix well and cook for about 15 minutes, on a low temperature, until the water evaporates. Stir constantly. After about 15 minutes, when all the water has evaporated, remove from heat.

Wash and drain mushrooms. Place them in small baking dish and spread tomato sauce over it. Salt and pepper to taste.

Preheat the oven to 300 degrees and bake for about 10-15 minutes.

Nutritional values per 100g:

Carbohydrates 10g

Sugar 2.4g

Protein 17.5 g

Total fat 4.8g

Sodium 161.4 mg

Potassium 31.5mg

Calcium 11mg

Iron 5.9mg

Vitamins (vitamin A; B-6; B-12; C; D; D2; D3; K; Riboflavin; Niacin; Thiamin; K)

Calories 112

39. Healthy bacon and vegetable frittata

Ingredients:

3 large slices of bacon

1 cup of leek, roughly chopped

2 large tomatoes, chopped

1 cup of spinach, chopped

6 eggs

2 egg whites

1 small avocado, sliced

¼ cup of fresh parsley, chopped

low fat oil spray

½ tsp of salt

¼ tsp of pepper

Preparation:

Spray some oil over a medium saucepan. Heat it up over a medium temperature and add bacon slices and leek. Fry for few minutes, until leek has softened. Now add tomatoes and chopped spinach and cook for another 4-5 minutes, until all the liquid evaporates and the vegetables soften.

Meanwhile beat the eggs and combine them with egg whites. Add salt and pour this mixture into the frying pan. Mix well with the vegetables and fry for about 3 minutes, stirring constantly.

Remove from the pan and serve with avocado slices. Sprinkle fresh parsley on top.

Nutritional values per 100g:

Carbohydrates 20.1g

Sugar 8.5g

Protein 21.3 g

Total fat 7g

Sodium 268mg

Potassium 73.3mg

Calcium 22mg

Iron 5mg

Vitamins (vitamin A; B-6; B-12; C; D; D2; D3; K; Riboflavin; Niacin; Thiamin; K)

Calories 160

40. Avocado tofu

Ingredients:

3 medium ripe avocados, cut in half

1 cup of soft tofu

3 tbsp of olive oil

2 tsp of dried rosemary

salt and pepper to taste

Preparation:

Preheat oven to 350 degrees. Cut avocado in half and remove the flesh from the center. Place 1 tbsp of soft tofu in each avocado half and sprinkle with rosemary, salt and pepper. Grease the baking pan with olive oil and place the avocados. You want to use a small baking pan so your avocados, fit tightly. Place in the oven for about 15-20 minutes.

Nutritional values per 100g:

Carbohydrates 22.3g

Sugar 6.1g

Protein 23.1 g

Total fat 6g

Sodium 428.1 mg

Potassium 73.2mg

Calcium 33mg

Iron 5mg

Vitamins (vitamin A; B-6; B-12; C; D; D2; D3; K; Riboflavin; Niacin; Thiamin; K)

Calories 167.5

41. Seitan and spinach omelet

Ingredients:

½ cup of soft tofu, pureed

½ cup of cannellini beans, pureed

1 cup of fresh spinach

5 thick slices of seitan

¼ cup of non fat milk

1 tbsp of olive oil

1/8 tsp of ground red pepper

¼ tsp of salt

Preparation:

Grease the frying pan with olive oil. Heat up over to medium-high heat. Meanwhile, whisk together pureed soft tofu, pureed cannellini beans, spinach and non fat milk. Pour into pan and stir for 3-4 minutes. Add seitan slices, ground pepper and salt. Turn off heat, but keep the pan on burner until seitan is heated.

Nutritional values per 100g:

Carbohydrates 12g

Sugar 2 g

Protein 11g

Total fat 3.4g

Sodium 166.9 mg

Potassium 73.1mg

Calcium 21mg

Iron 5.1mg

Vitamins (vitamin A; B-6; B-12; C; D; D2; D3; K; Riboflavin; Niacin; Thiamin; K)

Calories 146

42. Pureed prunes whites with tofu

Ingredients:

½ cup of pureed prunes

1 cup of pureed soft tofu

¼ cup of non fat milk

1 tbsp of oil

salt to taste

Preparation:

Combine pureed prunes with pureed soft tofu. Mash well with a fork and add some salt to taste – about ¼ tsp will be enough. Grease the frying pan with oil. Heat up over to medium-high heat. Pour this mixture into a frying pan and fry for 3-4 minutes, stirring constantly.

Nutritional values per 100g:

Carbohydrates 31g

Sugar 3.8g

Protein 27g

Total fat 6g

Sodium 412mg

Potassium 623mg

Calcium 171.7mg

Iron 0.83mg

Vitamins (Vitamin C total ascorbic acid; B-6; B-12; Folate-DFE; A-RAE; A-IU; E-alpha-tocopherol; D; D-D2+D3; Thianin; Niacin)

Calories 283

43. Sweet potatoes with agar powder

Ingredients:

4 medium sweet potatoes, peeled

2 tbsp of plain agar powder

2 medium onions, peeled

1 tbsp of ground garlic

2 tbsp of olive oil

½ tsp of sea salt

¼ tsp of ground pepper

Preparation:

First you need to disolve 2 tbsp of plain agar powder in 2 tbsp of water. Whip well and place in the refrigerator for 15 minutes.

Preheat your oven to 350 degrees. Spread the olive oil over a medium sized baking sheet. Place the potatoes on a baking sheet. Bake for about 40 minutes. Remove from the oven and allow it to cool for a while. Lover the oven heat to 200 degrees.

Meanwhile, chop the onions into small pieces. Take the agar powder out of the fridge. Whip well again. This will give you an egg whites substitute. Cut the potatoes into thick slices and place them in a bowl. Add chopped onions, egg whites, ground garlic, sea salt and pepper. Mix well.

Nutritional values per 100g:

Carbohydrates 18g

Sugar 9.8g

Protein 21g

Total fat 7g

Sodium 529mg

Potassium 63.1mg

Calcium 21mg

Iron 8.9mg

Vitamins (vitamin A; B-6; B-12; C; D; D2; D3; K; Riboflavin; Niacin; Thiamin; K)

Calories 120

44. Cranberry oatmeal

Ingredients:

1 cup of fresh cranberries

2 cups of rolled oats

1 tbsp of pumpkin seeds

1 medium apple, cut into slices

1 cup of almond Greek yogurt

½ cup of almond cream

½ cup of maple syrup

Preparation:

Preheat the oven to 350 degrees. Spread the pumpkin seeds in a baking sheet and toast for about 5-6 minutes. You want a nice lightly brown color.

Boil the cranberries over a high temperature. Cook until they burst. Add the oats, almond cream, apple slices and stir well. Cook for another 7 minutes, or until the oats are cooked. Stir in the pumpkin seeds. Remove from the heat and let it stand for 10 minutes. Serve cold with the almond yogurt and maple syrup.

Nutritional values per 100g:

Carbohydrates 25g

Sugar 13.2g

Protein 26.3 g

Total fat 11g

Sodium 575 mg

Potassium 92mg

Calcium 28mg

Iron 9.7mg

Vitamins (vitamin A; B-6; B-12; C; D; D2; D3; K; Riboflavin; Niacin; Thiamin; K)

Calories 194

45. Chia seeds pate

Ingredients:

½ cup of chia seeds powder

¼ cup of chia seeds

½ cup of soft tofu, pureed

3-4 cloves of garlic

¼ cup of non fat milk

1 tbsp of mustard

¼ tsp of salt

Preparation:

Chop the garlic and mix with mustard. In a large bowl, combine soft tofu with non fat milk, salt, chia seeds powder and chia seeds. Mix well and add garlic and mustard. Allow it to stand in the refrigerator for about an hour before serving. It can be kept in the refrigerator up to 10 days.

Nutritional values per 100g:

Carbohydrates 13g

Sugar 5.5g

Protein 19.3 g

Total fat 4g

Sodium 363.2 mg

Potassium 82.1mg

Calcium 21mg

Iron 4.3mg

Vitamins (vitamin A; B-6; B-12; C; D; D2; D3; K; Riboflavin; Niacin; Thiamin; K)

Calories 134

46. Soft tofu with green peppers

Ingredients:

½ cup of soft tofu, pureed

2 small green peppers, chopped

¼ tsp of red pepper

¼ tsp of sea salt

1 tbsp of olive oil

Preparation:

Combine soft tofu with red pepper and sea salt and mix well using a fork.

Heat up the olive oil over to medium-high heat and fry the chopped green peppers for about 10 minutes. Add tofu, stir well and fry for another 3 minutes. Remove from the heat and serve.

Nutritional values per 100g:

Carbohydrates 12.1g

Sugar 4.5g

Protein 15 g

Total fat 4g

Sodium 263.mg

Potassium 81 mg

Calcium 11mg

Iron 3mg

Vitamins (vitamin A; B-6; B-12; C; D; D2; D3; K; Riboflavin; Niacin; Thiamin; K)

Calories 111

47. Walnuts and strawberries salad

Ingredients:

½ cup of ground walnuts

2 cups of fresh strawberries

1 tbsp of strawberry syrup

2 tbsp of coconut cream

1 tbsp of brown sugar

Preparation:

Wash and cut the strawberries into small pieces. Mix with ground walnuts in a bowl. In a separate bowl, combine strawberry syrup, coconut cream and brown sugar. Beat well with a fork and use to top the salad.

Nutritional values per 100g:

Carbohydrates 19g

Sugar 7.5g

Protein 22g

Total fat 5.8g

Sodium 532 mg

Potassium 83mg

Calcium 31.3mg

Iron 7mg

Vitamins (vitamin A; B-6; B-12; C; D; D2; D3; K; Riboflavin; Niacin; Thiamin; K)

Calories 186

48. Apple salad recipe

Ingredients:

1 large apple

1 cup of chopped spinach

1.5 cup of sweat cream

1 tbsp of apple juice

½ cup of lentil

1 tsp of apple vinegar

Preparation:

Wash and peel the apple. Cut it into thin slices. Use a large bowl to combine the apple with other ingredients. Season with apple vinegar and serve cold.

Nutritional values per 100g:

Carbohydrates 16.1g

Sugar 2.5g

Protein 23.5 g

Total fat 5g

Sodium 567.1 mg

Potassium 84.2mg

Calcium 33mg

Iron 9.4mg

Vitamins (vitamin A; B-6; B-12; C; D; D2; D3; K; Riboflavin; Niacin; Thiamin; K)

Calories 198

49. Spinach omelet

Ingredients:

½ cup of pureed prunes

1 cup of baby spinach leaves, chopped

1 tbsp of onion powder

¼ tsp of ground red pepper

¼ tsp of sea salt

1 tbsp of tofu, grated

1 tbsp of flaxseed oil

Non fat milk, optional

Preparation:

Combine pureed prunes with baby spinach leaves and grated tofu. Beat well with a fork. Season with onion powder, red pepper and sea salt.

If your mixture is too thick, you can add some non fat milk.

Heat up the olive oil over a medium heat. Add egg mixture and fry for 2-3 minutes.

Spread this mixture over a baking sheet and bake for another 15-20 minutes at 200 degrees.

Nutritional values per 100g:

Carbohydrates 18.1g

Sugar 6.1g

Protein 17.5g

Total fat 3g

Sodium 112mg

Potassium 43.3mg

Calcium 19mg

Iron 6mg

Vitamins (vitamin A; B-6; B-12; C; D; D2; D3; K; Riboflavin; Niacin; Thiamin; K)

Calories 97

50. Fried eggs with chopped mint

Ingredients:

3 eggs

1 tbsp of olive oil

1 tbsp of chopped mint

1 cup of cherry tomatoes

1 small onion

pepper to taste

salt to taste

Preparation:

Cut the vegetables into small pieces and fry in large saucepan on a low temperature for about 15 minutes. Wait for the water to evaporate. Beat the eggs and add chopped mint. Mix with vegetables, add olive oil and fry for few minutes. Before serving add some salt and pepper to taste.

Nutritional values per 100 g:

Carbohydrates 8.1g

Sugar 4g

Protein 28g

Total fat (good monounsaturated fat) 11.9g

Sodium 176mg

Potassium 174mg

Calcium 17.9mg

Iron 1.5mg

Vitamins (vitamin A; B-6; B-12; C; D; D2; D3; K; Riboflavin; Niacin; Thiamin; K)

Calories 194

51. Veal chop with chopped cloves

Ingredients:

2 large veal chops

1 cup of chopped cloves

4 tbsp of olive oil

1 tbsp of dried parsley

1 tsp of rosemary

1 tsp of red pepper

1 tbsp of lemon juice

Preparation:

Mix well the cloves, olive oil, parsley and rosemary to get a nice sauce. Wash the steak and put it in a small baking tray. Add sauce and bake for 15-20 minutes at 300 degrees. Remove from the oven, sprinkle with pepper and lemon juice. Decorate with few parsley leaves. Allow it to cool for about 10 minutes.

Nutritional values per 100g:

Carbohydrates 8.2g

Sugar 4.9g

Protein 22g

Total fat 9.6g

Sodium 97.2 mg

Potassium 381mg

Calcium 4.5mg

Iron 5.3mg

Vitamins (vitamin A; B-6; B-12; C; D; D2; D3; K; Riboflavin; Niacin; Thiamin; K)

Calories 216

OTHER GREAT TITLES BY THIS AUTHOR

www.ingramcontent.com/pod-product-compliance
Lightning Source LLC
Chambersburg PA
CBHW071740080526
44588CB00013B/2109